When nighttime brings forth all its stars and moonbeams,

I sleep well at night, and I have pleasant dreams.

I close my eyes, drift off at night, into a sleep so deep.

I awaken happy and refreshed in the morning, Because of my good night's sleep.

Ha ha ha, ha ha ha, ha ha ha

I love to laugh. I love to dance and sing. I love the beauty of nature, I love all living things.

Others praise me often.

I always do my best. It's not if you win that matters, I suppose you know the rest.

Others believe in me, And when all is said and done, We're never really far apart, Because, You and I are One.

Praise me, believe in me...

I enjoy music, I enjoy dancing.

I like to read. It's like growing a plant, Or planting a seed. I've been told that, I am loved deeply, Wherever I may go.

And though it's nice for you to say, It's important that I know.

Learning is fun. My mind is quick. I am a ... times, that is the trick!

I remember things easily. Because, I pay attention. I like to be read to, Did I happen to mention?

I like myself, I believe in me, I am calm and relaxed, I am the best me That I can be.

I love myself, I believe in me...

I am balanced, I am joyful.

And, My soul...

I am Loved, I am lovable.

I love life More and more each day

What more can I say?

I am at peace within myself.

A gift my soul shall bring, I am one with everyone, I am one with everything!

Affirmations for Children

www.iamalovableme.com

Publisher's Cataloging-in-Publication
(Provided by Quality Books, Inc.)

Penchina, Sharon.
I am a lovable me:affirmations for children/
Sharon Penchina and Stuart Hoffman.
p.cm.
SUMMARY: Collection of illustrated affirmations in rhyme format
for children and intended to aid in building a strong self image.
Audience: Ages 0-7.
LCCN 2003095465
ISBN 0-9740684-5-4

1. Self-esteem in children--Juvenile literature.
[1. Self-esteem.] I. Hoffman, Stuart (Stuart E.) II. Title.

BF723.S3P46 2004   158.1'083
QBI33-1603

Printed in China

I AM a Lovable ME!

By Sharon Penchina C.Ht. & Dr. Stuart Hoffman

For
~Justin & Jacob~
~Jordan, Eric and Brandon~
And the Lovable ME in everyone!

2 Imagine
Scottsdale, Arizona
United States of America

DID YOU KNOW??

- There are almost 100 affirmations in this book.

- Affirmations are positive, empowering statements.

- Affirmations promote optimistic self talk.

- They promote positive action.

- Positive affirmations build self confidence and self esteem.

- Positive affirmations create positive pictures in our minds.

- Affirmations are most powerful when we:
    Say them in the present tense.
    Write them down.
    Feel them strongly.
    Say them everyday.

- Affirmations form our behavior patterns and habits.

- They are the foundation of our internal dialog.

- Affirmations help us focus our thoughts in a healthy way.

- Affirmations promote positive thinking.

"Our internal dialog
has more to do with
our success in life
than any other factor."

Unknown

There's no denying, It's plain to see,

LOVABLE ME

I have to admit, I am a Lovable Me!

I am happy to say,
I am pleased to shout,
I am light, I am love,
I am beautiful inside and out.

Once you meet me,
I am sure you will find,

I am unique, I am special, I am one-of-a-kind..........

I smile a lot, I stand straight and tall.

I am proud of myself,

I am loved, after all.

LOVABLE ME

My light shines bright, for the whole world to see!

I give love to others, and it comes back to me.........

I am fun to be with,
I am awesome,
I am smart,
I make friends easily,
Because, I come from my heart!

I like to help others,
That's the best way to be,
I am patient,
I am peaceful,

I am joyful in all things.

And truly, I am at ease.
I get along well with others,
And I'm really quite easy
to please.

You can count on me,
on me you can depend.
I share my toys with others,
and I am a very good friend.

I enjoy meeting new people!
There is no doubt,
That friends and family,
Are what it's all about.

I love my family,
I'm glad we're together.

My family loves me,

Right now and forever.

I am thankful
for my family,
And the way they care for me.
They smile, and hug,
and love me so,
Which makes me so hap-py!

I am healthy, I am strong.
I enjoy being myself.

And I have all along!

Lovable me

I rest when I'm tired

ZZZZ

I eat foods that are
good for me,
I am happy,
I am healthy,
and as strong
as I can be.

I drink lots of fresh water,

That keeps my body strong.

I can jump so high-nearly touch

the sky and run for oh, so long.

I breathe in and out deeply,
all throughout the day,

Which makes it easy
to rest or sleep,
and so much easier
when I play.

When nighttime brings forth all its stars and moonbeams, I sleep well at night, and I have pleasent dreams.

I close my eyes,
drift off at night,
into a sleep so deep.

I awaken happy
and refreshed in the morning,
Because of my good night's sleep.

I am creative,
I love learning
new things,
Pretending and
imagining,
That's when
My heart sings!

creative

imagination

I have a great imagination,
Pretending what or who to be.
Most of all I'm pleased to say,

I am happy to be me.

ha ha ha ha ha ha

I love to laugh,
I love to dance and sing,
I love the beauty of nature,
I love all living things.

ha ha ha

I like myself,

I believe in me,

I am calm and relaxed,

I am the best me

That I can be.

I am always confident,

I am a winner .... it's true,

always try my best,

At whatever I do!

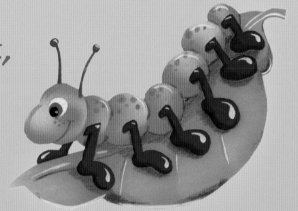

Learning is fun, My mind is quick, I am a good listener, That is the trick!

I remember things easily,

Because, I pay attention.

I like to be read to,

Did I happen to mention?

I enjoy music,
I enjoy dancing.

I like to read.
It's like growing
a plant,
Or planting a seed.

I've been told that,

I am loved deeply,

Wherever I may go,

And though it's nice for you to say,

It's important that I know.

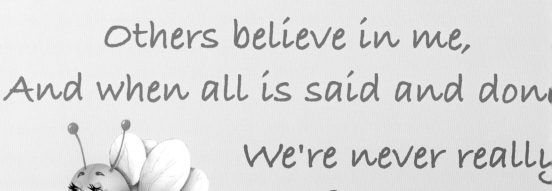

Others praise me often,

I always do my best.
It's not if you win that matters,
I suppose you know the rest.

Others believe in me,
And when all is said and don[e]

We're never really
far apart,
Because,
You and I are One[.]

Praise me...Believe in me...

I light

You can't help but see,
I radiate Light,
That grows larger
and larger,
And always shines
bright.

the world.

I bring happiness to
those who seek,
The light within
themselves that grows,
Brighter every day
and every week.

I love myself, I believe in me!

I am balanced,
I am joyful,

And, My soul is free.

I am at peace within myself,

A gift my soul shall bring.
I am one with everyone,
I am one with
everything!

I am love

I love life,

More and
more each day,

What more
can I say?

There's no denying, it's plain to see,

LOVABLE ME

I have to admit, I am a Lovable Me.

I smile a lot, I stand straight and tall.
I am proud of myself,
I am looked after all.

LOVABLE ME

My light shines bright, for the world to see.
I give love to others, and it comes back to me.

I am unique, I am special,
I am one-of-a-kind.

Once you meet me,
I am sure you will find,

You can count on me,
On me you can depend.
I share my toys with others,
and I am a very good friend.

I am fun to be with,
I am awesome,
I am smart,
I make friends easily,
Because, I come from my heart!

I like to help others,
That's the best way to be,
I am patient,
I am peaceful,

I am free to be me!

I enjoy meeting new people!
There is no doubt,
That friends and family,
Are what it's all about.
I love my family,
I'm glad we're together.

My family loves me,

Right now and forever.

I am creative
I love learning
new things,
Pretending and
imagining,
That's when
My heart sings!

imagine

creative

I have a great imagination,
Pretending what or who
Most of all I'm pleased to be
I am happy to be me